Congratulations on being accepted to college! This is sure to be an exciting time, full of new adventures, and many "firsts". One important new responsibility will be independently managing your money.

You may find there is a lot of information that your parents forgot to tell you. This guide is here to help! It is filled with expert advice, quick tips, helpful resources and real life examples to help you get your head around managing money. It will show you how to skillfully avoid common mistakes and build good financial habits that will last your whole life.

This book will take just a short time to read, but it will show you how to save thousands of dollars in the long run. It just might be the best college course you never registered for! And once you put into practice what you learn here, you'll not only be "in the money", but you'll soon be getting high-fives from your friends, friend requests from the bursar and the total respect and admiration from your parents that you've always dreamed of. *OMG!*

O.M.G.

OFFICIAL MONEY GUIDE FOR
COLLEGE STUDENTS

CONTENTS

What's This Going to Cost?

Know What You're Dealing With.

One of the many mysteries of college, especially freshman year, is what being there is actually going to cost you. Sure, you know there's tuition. If you're living in a dorm, there's room and board. Those bills arrive before you ever set foot on campus.

But how much will you need to make it through the first semester, let alone the first year? That's not so clear.

Here's what to plan for first: the start-up costs of being a college student.

MESSY MONEY MOMENT

RECEIPT REGRETS: MICROWAVE MELTDOWN

You splurged and bought a new microwave for your dorm room. But when you show up with your stuff on the first day, turns out you're actually not allowed to have a microwave in your room. And, you didn't keep the receipt, so there's no way to return it and get your money back.

Receipts may seems like a waste of time—another scrap of paper in your pocket or another email clogging up your inbox. But it's important to keep all your receipts for new stuff until you're fully moved in and know what you'll really need. Otherwise, you've spent part of your budget on things you can't use. In fact, keeping receipts and records of your purchases is always a good idea, so you can prove what you paid for something in case you want to return or exchange it, or if the item turns out to be faulty in some way.

⏻ STARTING UP

Typical start-up costs include the items listed here. Some things, like a laptop, you may already have, which can help reduce the cost of your pre-school shopping.

Laptop
Tablet
Software for specific courses
Textbooks
Class, lab, and studio fees
Bedding and towels
Fridge and other appliances

It's always great to avoid buying something that you'll only need for a year or two. For example, you may want to consider borrowing those extra-long twin sheets you'll need from a sibling or another student who's moved off-campus.

🥤 EVERYDAY COSTS

Here's a heads up: You'll probably be amazed at how fast cash can disappear if you've never lived on your own before.

Say you're starving when you finally finish a paper and the only thing in your fridge is a Diet Coke. You can't pay for pizza delivery with your meal card, so it's down to what's left of your cash or another hit on your debit card.

Here are some other day-to-day things you'll most likely end up spending money on:

Toiletries like toothpaste and shampoo
Other drugstore purchases
Laundry
Coffee and snacks
Cleaning supplies
Event tickets

Some costs are fixed by the contracts you sign—like your phone agreement and your rent if you're living off campus. It works in your favor that

Fixed Vs. Variable

these costs are the same amount every month, because you can plan for them. But if you don't pay them in full, you'll eventually find yourself without a phone, or much worse, with no place to stay.

There are often ways to reduce fixed costs. For example, staying on your family's phone plan may be cheaper than having your own account, provided the service is good in both locations. Adding another roommate will reduce your rent (though it might be a little crowded).

Other costs are variable, and change from month to month. You've got a little more flexibility with these costs—like food and clothing—since you can always cut back if you're running short of cash. One solid way to reduce costs is to get serious

about sustainability. Refilling a water bottle is cheaper than buying bottled water AND way better for the environment.

It may also be harder than ever to walk the line between what you want and what you need, especially if your new friends—or some of them at least—never seem to think twice about going out to dinner or paying a $10 cover to hear a band.

 TIP: It never hurts to ask in the Financial Aid or Bursar's office if some fees can be waived or reduced if they're a serious hardship for you.

> # *You need to know who is going to pay for what.*

📖 SO WHO PAYS?

If your parents are planning to help you out financially while you're at school, you need to know who is going to pay for what. The best time to have that conversation is before you start your first semester.

What you work out with them may change throughout your time in college. And it may not be the same deal that your friends have with their families. But it will have a major impact on your spending decisions.

ON THE MAP

Everyday costs also vary by geography—so where your school is matters. Living in some places (think rural versus a big city) is just cheaper than living in others. Sometimes a lot cheaper.

For example, are they going to pay for all the purchases you make with your school-issued debit card, or is that on you?

MAJOR MONEY MOMENT

REDUCE WASTE, REDUCE COSTS: GOOD HABIT TO HAVE

You decide that it's time to get your roommates on board with your plan to be kinder to the planet. With a little urging, you get everyone to turn off lights when they leave, only run the dishwasher when it's full, and put on a sweatshirt instead of cranking the heat. Guess what? When the utility bills come at the end of the month, you've saved the household close to $100.

Being green can have the added benefit of really bolstering your budget. If you get in the habit of not using electricity, water, and other resources you don't actually need, that's a double win. Another earth-friendly habit that also saves you money? Some coffee shops offer a discount if you use your own cup.

How Do I Keep My Expenses Under Control?

Design a Budget.

So now that you have an idea of what kinds of expenses you might have, you can think about how to manage them. **Successfully balancing your spending, otherwise known as managing your money, gives you financial control.** Managing money doesn't mean spending until it's all gone, or hoping that it will last until you get some more. It means being in charge of what you spend. For that, you need a plan, also known as a budget.

With a budget, you compare the money you've got with the expenses you need to cover. Then you figure out how to make them come out even.

Start by listing all the money that you have available to spend: money you've saved to cover living expenses, money you get from home, and money you're earning.

HINT: It's easier to budget by the month than for the full academic year. So if you have $2,500 in your savings account, divide by nine and allocate $278 to your monthly income.

Then record your expenses. If you're not sure where all the money is going, you're definitely not alone. But you can figure it out if you track everything you spend over a few weeks. You can do it old-school, on paper, or you can choose one of the many apps that let you record expenses on the go. *(See Resources)*

It's important to be specific when you record your spending, even if the amounts seem inconsequential— like $3.25 for coffee, $35 for roomie's b-day present, $12 for laundry. Then when you sit down to build your budget, you'll have the info you need.

 AN EXPENSE INVENTORY

You'll definitely want to budget for:

- Food not covered by your meal plan
- Books and school supplies
- Clothing
- Cell phone bill
- Entertainment
- Transportation
- Laundry and cleaning supplies

GET THINGS IN BALANCE

What if it turns out you're spending more than your income for the month? You can either beef up what's coming in, or trim down what's going out. Ideally, you can do a little of both.

Usually coming up with more income means finding a job or adding shifts to your existing one. Yes, your hours at work mean time away from studying, sports, and hanging out. But it's worth it to have a positive money balance.

Cutting back on spending? You probably can't do anything to bring down the fixed costs. But you're definitely in control when it comes to other ones. **It can help to choose one thing that you usually spend money on, and just say no.** That can be easier than trying to shave a little bit off a lot of different expenses. For example, stop skipping lunch in the dining hall (already paid for by your meal plan!) and buying it instead in the student union café.

While it's always nice to have some money left over at the end of the month, that's probably less important now than it will be after graduation. So don't sweat it if you're hitting your budget to the dollar every month. *What's non-negotiable now?* Consistently spending more than you can afford.

- Toiletries, prescriptions, and haircuts

- Gifts

If you're living off campus, include rent, utilities, and renter's insurance if your parents aren't picking up those costs. If you have a car, include gas and parking, plus insurance and loan payments if you're responsible for them.

As you can probably guess, living in your own place can be much more expensive than living in a dorm. That's an important thing to consider when you're thinking about where to live.

Monthly Spending Plan

INCOME

FIXED INCOME	Projected	Actual		FLEXIBLE INCOME	Projected	Actual
Job 1				Job 1		
Job 2				Job 2		
Scholarship/ Grants				Parents/Relatives		
Loans/Refund check				Cash gifts		
ESA/529 Plan				Other		
Other savings				Subtotals		
Other						
Subtotals						

COSTS

SAVINGS	Projected	Actual		FOOD	Projected	Actual
Savings				Groceries		
Emergency Fund				Snacks		
Other				Coffee		
Subtotals				Eating out		
				Other		
ON-CAMPUS COSTS	Projected	Actual		Subtotals		
Residence hall						
Meal plan/ Flex funds				**PERSONAL CARE**	Projected	Actual
Parking pass				Medical		
Student health insurance				Personal hygiene		
Other				Clothing/Shoes		
Subtotals				Laundry		
				Health club		
SOCIAL	Projected	Actual		Other		
Cellphone				Subtotals		
Movies						
Music				**GIFTS AND DONATIONS**	Projected	Actual
Gaming				Charity 1		
Sports events/ Concerts				Charity 2		
Gifts				Other		
Subtotals				Subtotals		

SCHOOL EXPENSES	Projected	Actual
Tuition		
Books		
Supplies		
Organization dues		
Lab fees		
Student loan interest		
Other		
Subtotals		

OFF-CAMPUS HOUSING	Projected	Actual
Rent/Mortgage		
Electricity		
Gas		
Water/Waste removal		
Cable/Satellite/Internet/Phone		

PROJECTED MONTHLY INCOME		
	Fixed Income	
	Flexible Income	
	Total Monthly Income	

ACTUAL MONTHLY INCOME		
	Fixed Income	
	Flexible Income	
	Total Monthly Income	

Maintenance or repairs		
Renters insurance		
Household supplies		
Subtotals		

TRANSPORTATION	Projected	Actual
Bus/Taxi fare		
Vehicle payment		
Insurance		
Parking		
Gas		
Maintenance		
Other		
Subtotals		

CREDIT CARD PAYMENTS	Projected	Actual
Credit card 1		
Credit card 2		
Other		
Subtotals		

TOTAL PROJECTED COST	
TOTAL ACTUAL COST	

PROJECTED BALANCE (Projected income minus projected cost)	
ACTUAL BALANCE (Actual income minus actual cost)	

Compare the numbers in the Projected Balance and Actual Balance columns in the green box above. If they are pretty close, great—they don't need to be exactly the same, to the penny. But if there is a big difference, and your Actual Balance is much lower than your Projected Balance, now's the time to rework this budget.

WORK OVERLOAD

You decided that you're tired of always being low on money, so you take on four more shifts at your job at the pizza place on campus. The bigger paycheck is awesome, but all the hours away from the library and your computer mean that you're not studying enough for tests and not submitting assignments on time. Plus, you're so tired after those late shifts cleaning up the restaurant that you've slept through a bunch of morning classes.

You end up failing two classes, which means you're not going to be able to earn enough credits to graduate on time. And paying tuition for a whole extra semester more than

wipes out the extra money you made at your job.

Cramming a lot into the day is part of the deal as a college student. The trick lies in devoting enough hours to the important things (classes and studying) while spending time at the necessary things (your job) so you do well at both.

 ## BUDGET FOR SAVING

What would happen to your budget if you had to give up your part-time job to take a required (non-paid) internship or your car unexpectedly needed work? Having an emergency fund in the bank would mean you didn't have to borrow to pay your bills.

But how can you possibly save now? Try trimming just a little bit from your flexible costs. Skip one dinner out. Pass up a concert. You get the idea.

In fact, including saving as an essential expense in your budget is a good start toward reaching financial goals. To make your good intentions a reality, set up an automatic transfer from your checking account to your savings account each month. It doesn't have to be much, but it should be something.

Heads Up: What isn't included in this budget are the tuition, fees, and room and board that are paid directly to your school as the term starts, either with financial aid credited to your account or by check or credit card.

 HOW MUCH WILL I REALLY NEED

Rough estimates for what you'll need fall somewhere between $770 and $1,150 a month*

Included in this amount are text-books, cable and phone bills, laundry, food, clothing, car expenses, and sometimes health insurance. It may

*(according to myfico.com and collegeboard.org)

turn out you spend even more, not less, from your second year on. That can happen if you move off campus, join the Greek system, or spend a semester abroad. But if you can find a rental that costs less than a dorm room and eat more cheaply than you would on a meal plan, you'll offset some of the added costs.

TIME IS MONEY

Time is a resource that's just as important as money, and it needs to be managed just as carefully. When you're in charge of your own schedule, it's remarkably easy to lose track of time, and how you spend it. Plus, there's so much going on that studying—or classes that meet at inconvenient times, like early in the morning—sometimes lose out.

Making smart use of your time is strikingly similar to budgeting your

funds. When you do it right, it makes life a lot less stressful.

But how DO you budget time? The key is figuring out a workable balance between what you have available—technically 24 hours a day—and what you do with each of those hours. Just like with your money budget, you can plot this out in a notebook, or use an app.

(See Resources)

WHERE TIME AND MONEY COLLIDE

There are ways that budgeting money and budgeting time overlap. If you want to graduate within a certain number of semesters (typically eight), you'll need to accumulate the number of credits your school requires to earn your degree.

Being short a required course or two could mean having to enroll for—and PAY for—an extra semester. That's why it's critical to plot out a workable plan for taking the courses you need, and balancing your other time commitments, like a job.

ᗡ CAN I AFFORD THAT?

Here are some estimated costs for some big-ticket items that may or may not have a place in your spending budget:

BUYING ALL NEW BOOKS FOR YOUR COURSES

$750

> **Cheaper option:** Source used copies of the books online or from students who have already completed the course. Rent the books, see if the books are available from the library—or even share with a classmate.

JOINING A SORORITY OR FRATERNITY

Ranges from several hundreds to over $1,000 (not including room and board)

> **Cheaper option:** Opt out of the Greek system. There are plenty of other ways to make great friends and be a part of a community on campus.
> Note that at some schools, over 75% of students are part of the Greek system, which is a factor to keep in mind when you're deciding which school is the right one for you.

FRATERNITY
PARKING
ONLY
←
VIOLATORS CITED/TOWED

HAVING A CAR ON CAMPUS

$500 to own and drive a car; as much as another $500 to park at school (less at some schools)

> **Cheaper option:** Public transportation. Bike. Walk. Lots of larger campuses have their own free student shuttles. There's no doubt having your own ride can be super convenient, but it is extremely expensive.

SEMESTER ABROAD

$15,000 – $30,000
(About double a semester at your home school)

> **Cheaper option:** Travel during your breaks from school. You might even be able to volunteer at an overseas organization that will pay for your travel and living arrangements. But if you have your heart set on being an international student, special scholarships, grants, and fellowships ARE available for study overseas—if you can get funding, that can be a big help.

COMPARE THAT COST!

DORM ROOM	VS.	OFF-CAMPUS APARTMENT
Electricity and water paid for		Electricity and water your cost
Basic supplies (TP, lightbulbs) covered		You buy basic supplies; roommates may not pay their fair share
You're on campus		May need to pay for transportation to/from campus
Meals covered by meal plan (though a reduced plan may be available)		Groceries are a big cost; sharing food expense with roomies can be tricky (But having a kitchen means you don't need to pay for a full meal plan)
Room & board covered by financial aid package		Rental deposit and security your responsibility
Room only available during semester		Full-year lease may be required. If full-year lease is available, you can avoid summer rent if you plan to stay local between school years
		Sorority/Fraternity houses: dues/fees on top of rent

What If I Need To Make Money?

The Right Job Is Out There.

If you need more income to make the money going out match up with the money coming in, finding a part-time job on or near campus may be the way to go.

One thing's for sure: You won't be the only one. Somewhere between 70% and 80% of undergrads have jobs. As many as 40% work full-time while being full-time students, according to a 2015 Georgetown University study, **Learning While Earning.**

How many hours are you willing to work? You may run into the argument that working more than 15 or 20 hours a week will have a negative impact on your education. Flip side? **Practicing juggling your obligations can polish up your time management skills.**

MAKING IT WORK

Some organizations, like environmental protection groups or museums, can't afford to pay their interns. And you may not be able to afford to work for free. But some colleges have programs that provide stipends to students who land qualifying unpaid or low-paid internships. Investigate your options at the Career Center or Financial Aid office.

And the hidden benefit of a job cutting into your social life is that you'll be spending less on going out. That's almost as good as a bigger number on your paycheck.

Between 70% and 80% of undergrads have jobs.

 ## WHERE THE WORK IS

There's a lot to be said for a job on campus. It's close. Your boss is likely to appreciate the demands of classwork and cut you some slack occasionally. Ideally the job could be relevant to the career you're planning—an added plus.

For example, you may find an opening as a research or lab assistant for a faculty member whose work you admire. Or, you might put your tech skills to use in the IT center or work with kids in the college daycare center. Tutoring other students who are struggling with writing can bump your own skills up a level. And while being a resident dorm adviser can take some patience, it may help you score free room and board.

If there aren't opportunities on campus, or if you can find a better paying job in the local community, working in a nearby town can make

sense. It may be harder to ensure that your work hours don't conflict with your class schedule. And you should add the cost of commuting into the equation, in both time and money. (If you'll be driving, you may burn up most of your income at the gas pump.)

Distinguishing yourself in an off-campus job through hard work and reliability during the school year might also put you in the running for a full-time summer position— another big plus if you're planning to stay in town between school years, or even over longer breaks.

TIP: Most colleges have Career Centers that also provide information on all the student jobs and internships on campus and nearby. Might be worth it to drop by.

FEDERAL WORK STUDY JOBS

Getting a Federal Work Study job depends on the level of financial aid you need, as established by your FAFSA, and how much your college has to underwrite these jobs. So while this may be an option, it's not guaranteed. If you qualify, the job could be either on or off campus, and the number of hours you can work depends on the amount of your financial aid award. **Huge bonus alert: It's not a loan, so you don't have to pay it back, and you'll earn at least $7.25 an hour.**

MAJOR MONEY MOMENT

SAVINGS BUMP

Your budget has been seriously out of whack for the past semester, even though you took on an extra shift at your job in the campus bookstore. Taking a look at your spending record, you realize that you've been blowing through your cash eating out at restaurants, sometimes as much as 3 or 4 times a week. So instead, you start meeting up with friends AFTER eating at the dining hall (which is already paid for!) and within two months, the money you are spending is matching up with the money you are making.

First off, great job on keeping a spending record—those numbers made it pretty clear where you had to cut back. And second, nice work on choosing an expense to cut out, and staying with it. Eating out isn't the only expensive habit that can be hard on your budget. Other examples of costs to kick to the curb are: living off campus, shopping online for new clothes and other non-essentials, having a car on campus.

FINDING INTERNSHIPS

An internship is a temporary job that can last anywhere from a month to a full semester. A good internship can round out your resume and may boost your chances of landing a great job.

Internships can be paid or unpaid. Paid has more than just the obvious advantage of a paycheck. It's also because employers generally offer salaried internships to recruit high-quality employees. And if you can convert an internship into a full-time job, you're likely to command a higher initial salary than classmates who didn't go the internship route.

Some paid internships are open only to students who have finished junior year. But that doesn't mean you shouldn't look sooner. Narrowing in on a potential career early in your college career can help you formulate your game plan as you choose classes and think about a major.

Unpaid internships can be a valuable way to try out a certain type of job, learn more about the field of work you think you might want to enter, and also an excellent way to build connections. But at the end of the day, if you need to make money, an unpaid internship is probably not the best choice.

TIP: If you work 15 hours a week making $7.25 an hour—that's the federal minimum wage and the least most jobs can pay—you'll earn $108.75 before Social Security and income taxes are withheld. That should cover a trip to the drug store and grocery store—or a few nights out.

Will Student Loans Hang Over My Head Forever?

Not If You Borrow Only What You Absolutely Need.

Financial aid can add major stress to your life. First you worry about getting enough. Then you worry about paying it back. Not all of it, of course—just the loans. But that could be a crazy amount to manage on a starting salary.

Unless you have a full scholarship that covers all your needs for all four years, you'll have to reapply for financial aid each year. That means filling out the FAFSA and any additional forms your school requires. It's best to complete the forms as soon as you can. That way you won't risk missing a deadline and losing out on aid you could have received.

GRANTS AND SCHOLARSHIPS

Investigate what's available each year—and then find out if you're eligible. If you are, go for it.

Grants and scholarships are different from loans in one huge way: You don't have to pay them back.

Scholarships that help to cover freshman year costs are often (though not always) renewed, typically dependent on your maintaining a certain grade point average. But if you're nervous that you might lose

MAJOR MONEY MOMENT

WANT TO TEACH?

The federal government provides TEACH grants if you're in a high-need field and you agree to teach in a low-income school. High-need fields include math, science, foreign languages, bilingual education, reading, and others included in the annual *Teacher Shortage Area Nationwide Listing (Nationwide List).*

your current aid, or you think you should be eligible for a larger sum, it's up to you to defend your position. Your argument may be strictly financial, though a number of scholarships are based on merit rather than need.

Grants may be available through academic departments, professional organizations, and the states.

Student loans are a lot like frenemies—potentially beneficial and something you might come to depend on, but not without some risk and mistrust. You need to watch out for your own best interests.

RESOURCES		
Federal grants	Federal Student Aid	Studentaid.ed.gov
State grants	U.S Department of Education	http://www2.ed.gov/about/contacts/state/index.html
Scholarships	FinAid	http://www.finaid.org/scholarships/
		https://studentaid.ed.gov/sa/types/grants-scholarships/finding-scholarships

Heads Up: Most private loans can be expensive. Repayment policies may offer less flexibility than you need. Many require a co-signer who's obligated to repay if you don't. If your financial aid package, including federal loans, isn't enough, you might want to rethink your plans before you take a private loan to make up the difference.

FEDERAL LOANS

With federal Direct Loans, you apply for and take a new loan each year, often at a different interest rate than your previous loan or loans. The same process applies for a federal Perkins loan, if your school participates in that program—though the rate on a Perkins stays the same.

The only thing that changes with Direct Loans, other than the rate, is that you can borrow slightly more in your junior and senior years than you can for the first two.

SO ARE LOANS EVER A GOOD IDEA?

There's no right answer, and definitely no agreement on this question.

Loan advocates argue that if borrowing is the only way you can afford to get your degree, it's worth the cost. In other words, they put college loans firmly in the "good debt" column—though most agree that it's irresponsible to go more deeply into debt than is absolutely necessary.

Those who don't think loans are the way to go claim that there are workable alternatives that won't weigh you down with debt for the next 10 or 20 years. Part of this argument is that it makes much more sense to attend a public college or university in the state where you

Heads Up: If you don't choose a plan, you'll be assigned to the standard plan—even if that might require a payment that's too large for you to handle. So be sure to get in touch with your loan servicer to make the best choice for you.

There are ways to reduce the total you owe, from a tiny percentage as a reward for scheduling electronic payments to potentially significant amounts if you work for ten years in a qualifying occupation. Any reduction in what you'll owe is a step in the right direction.

live than enroll in a costly private college or out-of-state public institution.

The bottom line is that it's a decision you and your family have to make after comparing the full cost of attendance with the amount that you need to cover. *You can do a reality test using the Repayment Estimator* at studentloans.gov, using either your actual outstanding loan total or what you anticipate borrowing by the time you graduate.

LOAN REPAYMENT

The reality of loans is that you have to pay them back, starting six months after you graduate in the case of Direct Loans. Another catch? If you drop out of school or are enrolled less than half-time, the repayment clock starts ticking immediately. Unless you re-enroll at least half-time within the six month grace period, you must begin to pay.

What you owe will depend on the amount you've borrowed, the interest rate or rates that apply to those balances, and the repayment plan you choose. There are seven options, including the standard plan, an extended plan, a graduated plan, and four plans where your payment amounts depend on your income combined with other factors such as family size and where you live. *(See Resources)*

MESSY MONEY MOMENT 😳

NOT PAYING IT BACK

You know that part of the deal of your student loan is paying it back. Somehow, though, you just can't seem to make those payments.

Now it's been six months since your last payment, and guess what. Your non-payment is reported to the national credit bureaus, and your credit score plummets. Even worse, you're considered to be in default.

Being in default means all sorts of bad things—like you won't be eligible for any more financial aid, and some of your paycheck may be withheld by your employer to go towards repaying the loan.

23

HOW DOES FINANCIAL AID WORK?

Knowing how to navigate the process—and staying on top of all the details about your aid—can help make getting money to pay for school smooth sailing.

When you fill out the FAFSA, you get to choose up to 10 schools to receive your application. You'll want to contact each school's financial aid office to confirm you're interested and find out what else you need to do. Some may want you to fill out a separate aid application or have specific cut-off dates.

Each school has the opportunity to make you an offer. Once you receive all of the offers, around the time you get acceptance letters, it's time to weigh your options.

You can accept, or reject, any offer of aid. **The golden rule to keep in mind when making these decisions is borrow only what you absolutely need, only when it's definitely necessary.** Remember, you're only borrowing when you take a loan. Grants and scholarships never have to be paid back.

Take the free money first. Then the money you earn (as in a work-study). Then take loans with flexible terms and a choice of repayment plans. That would be federal Direct Loans and loans from your college or university—provided the rates and terms are acceptable to you. In final place are private loans, if they're absolutely necessary.

SHOW ME THE MONEY

The way your financial aid gets paid has to do with what type of aid it is. For example, a loan payment is different than a payment that you get for doing a work-study program.

Usually, you get your financial aid loan money in at least two payments, called disbursements. Often, the payments are tied to the school calendar. So you'll receive a disbursement every trimester or semester. You should get a written confirmation from your school's

financial aid office each time a disbursement is made.

Money goes first towards paying for the basics: tuition, related fees, and room and board (unless you live off campus). If there's any money left over, it will be paid to you. But remember, it's often a good idea to return that portion of the loan that you don't need for school, or have it credited to the next term's bill so you're not tempted to buy other things with it.

Heads Up: Returns allowed! You can cancel all or part of a federal student loan within 120 days of a disbursement if you end up not needing the money. You have to return the amount that was disbursed but you should not have to pay any interest or fees on that cancelled loan.

UNDERSTANDING YOUR LOAN

One surefire way to get into difficulty with your loans is losing track of them. It's essential to be familiar with the terms of your financial aid, including:

What you are borrowing

What you will need to repay, and when

Who the loan servicer is (also called the loan holder)

Who the loan guarantor is, if there is one

One reason it gets so complicated is that you're not taking just one loan to cover all four years: You take a new one every year. The amounts might change since the cost of attendance is likely to change, as is the interest rate. And the aid your school offers you can change too.

Just like with most other money matters, if you are confused or find yourself in trouble, don't ignore or postpone. Ask for help.

- Make an appointment with the financial aid office at your school.

- Go to the National Student Loan Data System (NSLDS) website, set up an account, and get the bottom line on your loans.

- Call the Federal Student Aid Information Center at 800-4-FED-AID.

- If you're having a dispute with your lender or financial aid office, call the US Department of Education Student Loan Ombudsman at 877-557-2575

A note on private loans: You'll have to keep track of those yourself. There's no database, or advocate, as there are for federal.

3 Parts of a Loan: What you are borrowing includes 3 things: the principal (the amount you borrow), the term (the length of time the loan lasts), and the interest rate (of the percentage of the principal you pay to borrow). With Direct Federal and most private loans there's also an annual fee for borrowing the money.

⚠ STUDENT LOAN SCAMS

You know the rules for avoiding scams and identity theft in everyday life—don't give out your personal and credit card information, don't believe offers that are too good to be true, don't be pressured into purchasing or signing an agreement.

Same's true here. There are companies that offer to help you find scholarships, fill out applications, get free financial aid money, and even help get you out of having to pay back your loans. At best, they're charging you for services that are actually free. At worst, they are stealing your credit card and other personal information to use for their own gain.

Be especially aware of companies that claim to help reduce what you owe on your loans, or promise to have your loans forgiven. And if a company says it will consolidate your loans so you make only one payment, forget it. You can consolidate Direct Federal Loans for free through the US Department of Education.

FINANCIAL AID TERMS TO KNOW

COST OF ATTENDANCE (COA)

Cost of attendance (COA) is an average cost that represents both the direct and indirect expenses of attending school over a given period of time. It's calculated by the school and includes tuition, fees, room and board, and allowances for books, supplies, transportation, loan fees, and some personal expenses. If you don't live on campus, an amount for housing and food replaces the amount for room and board.

Your cost of attendance helps to determine how much you are eligible to borrow in federal, institutional, and private loans.

DEFERMENT

A deferment temporarily suspends your federal student loan repayments. You may qualify if you are unemployed, are having certain other economic hardships, are returning to school at least half-time, or are on active or post-active military duty.

If the deferral is granted and you're enrolled at least half-time or on qualifying military duty, there is no time limit on a deferment. In other cases, you can defer payments for up to a total of three years.

DELINQUENCY vs DEFAULT

When you fail to make a payment on your loan by the due date, you are considered delinquent on the loan. When you have been delinquent about making payment for nine months, you are considered in default. Once you are in default, the entire loan balance becomes due.

FORBEARANCE

Forbearance lets you temporarily postpone repayment of your federal student loans, reduce the amount of each payment, or extend the repayment period. Forbearance requests are granted for a 12 month period and may be extended at expiration, for a total of three years.

GRACE PERIOD

With a federal student loan, the grace period is the amount of time between the date you graduate or fail to enroll at least half-time and the date your first loan repayment is due.

MASTER PROMISSORY NOTE (MPN)

A master promissory note is a legal agreement between you and your lender. By signing it, you agree to repay what you borrow. The note explains your rights and responsibilities as a borrower, how interest on your loan is calculated, and how you repay. Once you sign the MPN for a Direct Federal Loan it covers new loans for 10 years.

What Do I Need to Know About Debt?

Don't Let Debt Get the Upper Hand.

We've all been there. There's something you want to buy that you know you shouldn't, at least not right now. Because if you spend money on yet another pair of shower shoes, or an online premium cable package to share with your roomie, that's money that will be gone when you have to pay for the books you need for your classes.

While a cheap pair of shoes doesn't seem like a huge deal—especially if you're just swiping your charge card or waving your phone at the register—you can dig yourself pretty deep into debt if you make too many choices like this.

In addition to student loans, debt means owing a balance on a charge card or credit card that you don't have the money to pay off. In this scenario, if you don't have the money to pay for the new shoes AND your books, by buying both without actually having the funds to cover the purchases, you're creating debt.

When you don't pay your bills, two things happen, and they're both bad. The first bad thing is that unpaid bills get bigger, because late fees and interest charges are added to the original amount. The second bad thing is that if you don't pay at all, you put a major dent in your credit score, which is essentially the grade you get for the way you use credit. And, if this happens too often, you have to be prepared for your phone to be cut off or your credit card to be declined or revoked.

A bad credit score leaves school with you when you graduate. It can hurt your chances of finding a good job, or getting a good loan rate on a car or a house.

If you take out any student loans, that's debt that you must eventually repay. You can look at that debt as a form of investment, in your education and your future.

Even worse? It's probably not just your credit score that you are hurting. Chances are your parents or other adults in your life are ultimately responsible, as co-signers on a credit card or school charge card. That means their money, and their financial reputation, is also on the line.

GOT DEBT? DON'T FREAK OUT

The up side is that debt usually doesn't just happen all of a sudden. It builds over time. The down side is that it can snowball pretty quickly. So you have to put on the brakes and reverse direction.

Here are some clues that debt is becoming a problem:

- You can't pay your utility or service provider bills **in full**

- You regularly run out of money before your next infusion of cash (whether it's from a paycheck or from home)

- You have to borrow money from friends

- You are paying only the minimum amount due on credit cards (or worse, just ignoring the bills)

- You can't complete certain course requirements because you can't cover the extra expenses, like lab or studio fees

Heads Up: What is a credit score anyway? It's actually a number, on a scale of 850 (really good!) to 300 (very bad). The score is based on how you use credit, including how much you owe and how timely you are in paying your bills. Your credit score can often be found on your monthly credit card statement.

Remember, a bad credit score leaves school with you when you graduate. *(See Resources)*

✂️ ✄ -ᴠ- SO WHAT DO I DO?

If any of that sounds familiar, don't panic. When you feel you're in over your head when it comes to money, it's tempting to just think about something else and plan to deal with it another time. But just like papers that don't write themselves, debt doesn't take care of itself. And the longer you ignore it, the worse it gets. Take action!

1. Go back to that budget. (If you haven't created one, now's the time.)

2. Figure out which expenses are more than you anticipated. If your phone bill is high, change your plan and cut back your use. If you are spending too much at the student union or campus market, find a ride to a larger discount chain and stock up on cheaper generic versions of everything from shampoo to mac n' cheese.

3. Stop spending money on extras, like going out to dinner, road trips to team games, and new clothes

MAJOR MONEY MOMENT

NO ROADTRIP, NO REGRET

It's decision time—today is the last day to decide whether you're going on a roadtrip to visit your BF at another school. You're ready to text her that you're coming, but realize you should take a look at your funds first.

You realize you haven't paid off your bills this month—and you still have to pay the studio fee for sculpture class. Ignore all that, and go on the trip anyway? Nope, not this time. You decide to hit reverse on the path to debt. You'll see your BF over break.

You rock. Not only have you avoided going a few more miles down the road to debt, but you've made a really

smart spending decision. A few more of these, and you'll probably be able to pay off all your bills AND your class fees. Ultimately, much better than a roadtrip.

for special occasions. Difficult, but necessary. Most campuses offer free events with lots of giveaways that won't cost you anything—including food and activities.

4. If you can, increase your income. Adding even a few more hours a week at your job can really make a difference when you're battling the debt demon. And if you don't have a job yet, consider looking for one on or near campus that will fit into your schedule.

Once you slow down—or completely stop—the flow of money to things that aren't essential, you can put that money towards paying off your bills. Start with bills for things that you need, like utilities, especially if you live off campus and are paying for services like electricity. And make

AWESOME JOB IDEA

Most campus dining halls offer student employees a free or discounted meal during their shift. Get paid to eat lunch for free! Make sure you can reduce your meal plan by a few meals a week or month so you're not paying for the food you can get for free.

sure you're paying at least the minimum due on any credit cards.

If you pay as much as you can to get those bills off your back, you'll reduce your debt and your money stress. Being debt-free doesn't happen in the blink of an eye. You have to work on it. But you can conquer it.

GOOD DEBT. IS THAT A THING?

It's one of those things you might have heard that doesn't quite make sense—that some debt is good. Really?

All debt involves buying or doing things that you can't afford to pay for now in cash—things that are possible only if you borrow. But unlike the cost of a third pair of shower shoes, some debt is worth it.

What about investing in yourself by using loans to help pay tuition? College graduates make, on average, about $1 million more over their lifetimes than they would without a degree. And you can also deduct college loan interest off your taxes. More earning power and lower taxes—definitely in the good debt category.

What's the Best Way to Pay for That?

It Depends on What You're Buying.

The big bucks of a college education change hands behind the scenes. The checks your parents write, the scholarships and grants you win, and the loans you take flow into your student account as the term begins and out again to pay tuition and fees, plus room and board if you're living on campus.

What's the best way to pay for the other stuff? That's in your hands.

Should you swipe your college ID card to pay for what you can? That probably includes food in the dining halls and campus markets, plus tickets to campus events like athletic games and concerts. It may work in the college bookstore too.

Maybe you're responsible for paying this bill, or maybe it goes right to your parents. Either way, it's real money that needs to be paid off.

CASH OR PREPAID PLASTIC

Should you pay cash for everything? It's true that using cash may help you put the brakes on spending because you're literally watching your money disappear. On the other hand, if you're trying to budget by tracking your spending, it's easy to lose count of what cash pays for. Once it's gone, it's hard to remember exactly where it went.

There's also the argument that cash is easy to lose and tough to recover.

So what about prepaid reloadable debit cards? Just like with cash, you simply can't spend more than you have, which is the balance on the card. If you load the amount you've budgeted to spend for the month, that's it 'til next month. And they work just about everywhere.

But there are some negatives too. Many prepaid cards are also loaded with big fees: fees for adding value, using an in-network ATM, paying

bills, even for swiping the card. The trick is to find one that's mostly fee-free.

There are also fewer protections if your card is lost or stolen than there are with credit cards and regular debit cards. If somebody swipes your card, you may never recover the amount they spent. And you can't dispute charges for defective purchases or services you didn't receive, the way you can with a credit card.

MESSY MONEY MOMENT 😳

OVERDRAFT: NOT SO SMOOTH

You decide to check your bank statement, expecting everything to look okay. But it's not. You've got a $35 overdraft fee. How did that happen? Chances are you had signed up for overdraft protection on your debit card, and you weren't paying attention to your available cash and just kept on spending. That means the smoothie you just bought for **$5** actually cost you **$40**.

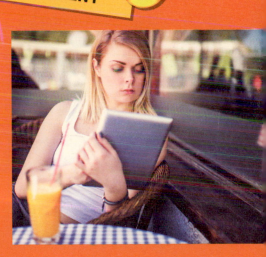

How to avoid this in the future? Keep better track of what you're spending by checking your balance frequently, and only spend what you actually have. The best option is getting rid of overdraft protection. Why? Because when you use it, you're essentially taking a loan to pay for everyday expenses. It's better to just watch your budget.

DEBIT OR CREDIT

If not cash or a prepaid debit card, then what? A different kind of debit card is available, one that allows you to pay by subtracting the amount directly from your checking account. And then there's credit.

Debit cards can be handy—whether you swipe, tap, wave your card at a card reader, or pay online, the amount you're spending comes straight from your account balance. It's also a plus that there's a record so you'll know where the money went.

You'll hear debit cards praised as a way to keep your spending under control and avoid the interest charges that can make using credit shockingly expensive.

So is using credit better? Only if you are disciplined about spending and realistic about having the money to always pay your outstanding balance in full and on time by the day it's due. That's the only way to avoid interest charges. And they can be killers. *Remember, when you use credit, it's really taking a loan.*

Emergency-use-only credit cards are a good thing to have, though. And if you're reserving a hotel room or renting a car, a credit card is better than a debit card. That's because when you use a debit card a hold is usually put on your account for the full potential cost of the transaction.

Heads Up: One option when using a debit card is to sign up for overdraft protection. This allows you to use money that you don't actually have in your account. In reality, you're borrowing it from the bank. *But you WILL end up paying: not only repaying the money that you borrowed, but also the sometimes very large overdraft fees.* You could be charged a $35 overdraft fee—or four $35 fees in the same day—if your balance is too low to cover your charges.

That cuts into your available balance. After the actual charge is debited, the hold may still be in effect. So you'll have to wait for it to be released and available in your account.

Using credit cards can work in your favor in another way—provided you make at least the minimum payment on time every month—because it helps you build a positive credit history. That's not such a big deal for now. But when you want to finance a car or a home, buy insurance, or get a job, your credit history will have a major impact on your application.

 ## LOAN MONEY IS NOT FOR PIZZA

It's a major mistake to spend federal student loans for anything but the direct costs of your education. While that usually means tuition, it can also include books or other materials you need for your classes. Here's the issue: After the federal aid you qualify for is credited to your student account—which typically happens twice an academic year—the college or university debits your account to cover tuition and fees. If there's money left over, and there often is, it's sent to you or deposited in your bank account unless you've made other arrangements. So basically it's yours to spend.

This is loan money. It will be included in the amount you have to repay eventually, plus interest. True, if your loan is subsidized, the interest charges haven't started yet. But they'll apply to the full amount of the loan once you begin to repay, even if you've spent the money on pizza and drinks.

The smartest choices you can make are either to leave the loan balance in your student account where it can be debited for future charges or send it back to the lender to reduce your debt. The Bursar's office or financial aid office can help you with that.

 # IS THAT DEAL REALLY A BARGAIN?

Stop. Think. Do the Math.

At school you're in charge of your own shopping decisions—groceries, stuff from the drug store, clothes and shoes, among other things. One of the big challenges is avoiding the trap of buying something you don't need—or more of something than you need—just because it's being pitched as a great deal.

It's the store's job to convince you to buy as much as possible. After all, that's how they make their money. But it's your job to figure out what you really need to buy, and avoid spending more than you need to pay.

In these circumstances, your best friend is simple math. If you can look through the special offer and see what the actual numbers are, it's often much easier to pass up a deal that doesn't work in your favor.

Doing the calculation can save you big bucks:

- What's the actual percentage discount I'm being offered?

- Will I really save money if I buy 2 instead of 1?

- If I buy something I can't really afford now with my credit card because it's on sale, and I end up paying interest on the purchase, will I actually save money?

Heads Up: The Temptation of Paying Electronically

Paying electronically is way too painless, especially when all you have to do is wave your phone at the register. But that can come back to bite you later if you forget that you're actually spending money.

That's not to say a digital wallet doesn't have benefits. Because you store all your credit and debit cards on your phone, you can check your account balances before you spend. You'll always know where you stand, financially speaking. And since the transactions are tokenized—which means they use a random series of numbers rather than your card number to pay—you're better protected against identity theft.

 ## DO THESE BARGAINS LOOK FAMILIAR?

BUY ONE, GET SECOND AT
50% OFF

Real deal? A 25 percent discount. And you probably only need one of whatever it is.

 ### IT'S ONLY A *ONE-TIME $35 FEE* IF YOU NEED TO OVERDRAW YOUR ACCOUNT.

Real deal? That fee translates to the ridiculous interest rate of 750% .

 ### 10% OFF ON YOUR PURCHASE WHEN YOU SIGN UP FOR A STORE CREDIT CARD.

Real deal? The APR is often very high—as high as 35% (average APR on a regular credit card is closer to 18%), so if you don't pay off the balance in full each month you'll be paying tons in interest. Plus, they make spending too much money in your favorite store way too easy!

BUY 2 FOR $7.00

Real deal? You don't need to buy two to get the same price. Just buy one for $3.50.

SHARING EXPENSES WITH ROOMMATES

When roommates share common expenses, such as rent, utility bills and household supplies, it works best if one person takes responsibility for being the household accountant, making sure that all bills are paid on time. Each roommate can give the accountant their share of the expenses to put into a separate checking account that is used exclusively for shared roommate expenses. The accountant should keep track of how much each person owes for each shared expense and the payments that are made. At the end of the semester, review the account together to see if anyone owes more, or is owed a refund.

How Does a Credit Card Really Work?

It's Called Revolving Credit.

Credit cards provide loans that are known as revolving credit. When you make a purchase with your credit card, you are borrowing money from the credit card company. As you repay the money you have borrowed, it is available to be borrowed again. The amount that the credit card company gives you access to is called your credit limit.

A credit limit can be small, like $500, or up to $10,000 or more, depending on lots of factors like if you've ever had a card before, how you've used cards in the past, and what your income is. If you use your card regularly and pay your bill every month, your limit usually goes up over time. But if you frequently pay late or miss payments completely, the card

MAJOR MONEY MOMENT

NOT MY CHARGE

You know it's a good idea to check your credit card statement to make sure all the charges look correct. So you take a peek. As usual, all looks fine…until you notice a charge for $120 at a sports store you would never buy anything from. You call the store first to let them know you didn't make that purchase. They won't agree to reverse the charge, but you don't give up that easily. Next call is to the credit card company.

Good move. Your card issuer will investigate the charge. You don't have to pay that part of your bill until they

look into it—and not at all if they decide in your favor. In most cases, the credit card company ends up agreeing that the card holder is not responsible for the questioned charge.

company may lower your limit or even cancel your card.

Every time you use the card, the amount you spend is deducted from your credit limit. When you repay an amount, it's available for you to borrow again. So say your credit limit is $1,000. You charge $550 on your card to buy a ticket home for the end-of-year break. If you repay all of that $550 when your bill is due, your available credit is $1,000 again.

But if you only pay $200, your available credit is $800, not $1,000. And if you end up owing interest because you don't pay in full and on time, that amount is subtracted from your available credit too.

If you try to spend more than your current credit limit, the purchase may be rejected. Worse yet, if it goes through,

you'll be charged an over-limit fee, often $25 for the first one and more if you do it again.

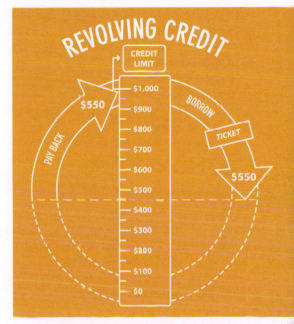

IT'S NOT YOUR MONEY

When you pay for something with a credit card, you are not using your own money. You are using the bank's money and you will need to pay it back sooner or later—preferably right away.

Heads Up: If you let those due dates slip by without paying too many times, the credit card company will raise your APR—if they don't just cancel the card. A higher APR makes the interest you owe even larger. The good news is that the higher APR is reversible over time if you consistently make on-time payments—but you have to call your credit card company and request a lower APR.

% INTEREST RATES

If you don't pay the full amount due, on time, you'll have to pay interest on your balance. The interest you owe is determined by the card's annual percentage rate (APR). An average rate is around 18%, which means you'll be charged 1.5% of any unpaid balance on your credit card each month. In the long term, that means that you'll end up spending more on your purchases than you initially thought you were paying—and definitely more than you needed too.

GRACE PERIOD

One convenient thing about revolving credit is something called a grace period, which most credit cards offer. That's the amount of time you have to pay a credit card bill before interest charges apply.

An example: You just got a new credit card. Your first bill of $275 is due on May 20th. If you pay the whole amount owed by the due date, any purchases you charge between when you got the bill and when it's due are interest free. So is anything you charge before the next bill is calculated.

But what if you'd made just the minimum payment on May 20th? Interest charges start applying to the unpaid balance right away. And any purchases you make are charged interest from the day you make them.

CARD DECLINED!
A REAL EMERGENCY

You've been racking up credit card charges, big and small, from a new guitar to game apps. Even worse, you haven't been keeping up with payments and you're dangerously close to your credit limit.

Then your car breaks down. This is what you were told the credit card was for—paying for real emergency expenses. You hand your card over to the garage owner, but you are over limit and the card is declined. Not only embarrassing, but now you can't cover your car repair.

Credit cards can be a lifesaver, but only if you keep your account in good working order. That means making careful spending decisions, not using it for things you want but don't need, and above all making sure you pay your bill—as close to the full amount owed as you possibly can. Then when an emergency rolls around, you've got the spending power to handle it.

DUDE, WHERE'S MY CARD?!

What happens if you lose your credit card and someone else uses it fraudulently? Your liability for unauthorized charges depends on whether it was your physical card or just your card number which was compromised. If your credit card is stolen and used to make unauthorized purchases, the bank cannot hold you liable for more than $50 in fraudulent charges. If a thief uses your card number by phone or the Internet, you have no liability. In either case, however, it's important to notify the bank as soon as you know that your card is missing. If you wait, the bank may not believe that the card was really lost or stolen.

With debit cards, which can also be used where Visa and MasterCard are accepted, you must act quickly when your card is lost or stolen in order to avoid liability for unauthorized charges. Your liability could be unlimited if you don't notify your bank in a timely manner. You should phone first, but official notice should always be given in writing.

How Do I Choose the Right Bank?

A Little Research Can Go a Long Way.

Where should you have your bank account, on campus or in your hometown? Or should you bank virtually with an online bank? To answer that question, first figure out what banking services you need (like access to free ATMs). Second, don't pay for anything you don't need.

All bank accounts are not created equal. The right one for you will help you manage money conveniently at the least possible cost.

That includes checking accounts, which you use to transfer money, whether online or by check, to other people or organizations, and savings accounts. You can't make payments from a savings account, though you can transfer money from it to your own checking account.

Accounts that offer the services you need but don't cost a lot are out there. Also, consider the pros and cons of a virtual bank or a credit union. They might be a better fit for you right now than a traditional bank.

ONLINE ACCOUNTS

Virtual banks and the online services of physical banks tend to be cheap and user-friendly if you're comfortable with handling everything—deposits, bill payments, transfers, withdrawals—or nearly everything, electronically.

The online banks you'll want to consider have vast networks of linked ATMs you can use without a fee or they automatically reimburse your fees (though sometimes there is a monthly cap on the number you're allowed).

Banking online means access to your accounts from anywhere there's a connection. But you'll want to avoid using public networks like in the campus coffeeshop, if possible. They make your account way too vulnerable to identity thieves.

TIP: Online banks have customer reps you can contact if there's a major disconnect between the money you think you have and what your online balance shows. If that happens, don't just wonder about it, look into it!

 IDENTITY THEFT

Identity theft stinks. It's when somebody steals your identity—using your Social Security number, your student ID number, or the PIN for your debit card—and uses it for financial gain. What makes losing money to ID theft even worse is that it can be hard to detect, and a hassle to clean up your financial records.

The potential for identify theft is why you should avoid using public wireless networks to log into any of your financial accounts. It's way too easy for an ID thief to access your account and use the information to steal your money.

The best way to handle identity theft is to prevent it. That means never sharing account numbers or PINs with anyone, including your roommates and your friends. If you have this information written somewhere, make sure it's not lying around for anyone to find. And make sure nobody is close enough to see your PIN when you enter it at an ATM or checkout register.

What might surprise you is that you have the smallest liability if an ID thief uses your credit or debit card. That's because if you report the card missing as soon as you realize it's gone, the most you can lose is $50.

One of the worst kinds of ID theft is when someone opens credit accounts in your name and borrows against those credit lines. You could be responsible for this debt unless you discover, and report, the theft promptly. That's why it's important to check your credit report once a year at annualcreditreport.com. It's free.

Heads Up: Also be aware that there are devices that can be attached to cash machines that can read the information you enter, mostly at non-bank ATMs. It might be a good reason to stick with bank ATMs, if you can.

Heads Up: Any account you use should be insured by the federal government, either through the Federal Deposit Insurance Corporation (FDIC) or the National Credit Union Share Insurance Fund (NCUSIF).

CREDIT UNIONS

It's easy to confuse a credit union with a bank: It also offers checking and savings accounts, takes deposits, and makes loans. But a typical credit union often charges less for the same services.

There are a few limitations. For one, credit unions have membership requirements. Sometimes, the bar is pretty low, such as living in a particular community. For others, eligibility may be restricted to employees of a particular organization and their families. But chances are if you're interested, there's a credit union for you.

You'll also find that some credit unions are small and have just a few branches, so they're not always convenient. But the larger ones, with good online services, might be worth checking out.

MAJOR MONEY MOMENT

BANKING BONUS: SAVING CASH

The bank account you opened when you first got to school as a freshman may not have been the best choice. It seemed fine at the time, but you seem to be owing a lot of fees that you hadn't expected—like every time you use an ATM that's not owned by your bank. You do a little looking online and realize that you could switch to a Student account—one that waives most fees and has a lower account balance requirement, and that ALSO reimburses you for any ATM usage fees.

While $3 here and there doesn't seem like a lot, there's no reason to pay those fees if you don't have to. And taking advantage of special account benefits and features for students is always a great way to go.

44

? QUIZ YOUR BANK

When you're looking for the right place to open a checking account, it's the questions you forget to ask that can end up costing you. An account that seems ideal can have hidden drawbacks—like fees for using your debit card or charges for online bill pay—that can wipe out any advantages they offer, like no monthly fee.

So be sure to find out:

- Is there a monthly maintenance fee? If so, is there a way to avoid it?

- Is a minimum balance required? How much is it? What happens if my balance is less than the minimum?

- Is there a special account available for students?

- Do I get a debit card? Is there a fee for using it? Is there a fee for a replacement card?

- How many ATMs does the bank have and where are they?

- Is there a fee for using the bank's ATM? What about ATMs at other banks or nonbanks, like the one in the local deli?

- Can I get reimbursed for withdrawals at ATMs not owned by the bank?

- Is there a fee for online bill pay?

- Do I get paper checks? Is there a per-check charge for using them?

- What are the overdraft charges? Can I arrange for overdraft coverage using a linked savings account? Can I refuse overdraft protection for my debit card but get it for checks and bills I pay electronically?

- Is there a mobile phone app to deposit checks remotely?

- Can I link my account to a digital wallet?

SCHOOL/BANK PARTNERSHIPS

If your school partners with a bank to offer low-cost checking accounts for students and staff, is that your best option? Maybe, but while some features may be free, you may find others that aren't. You should ask the same questions about fees—including overdraft coverage, online bill pay and ATM use—as you do of any other bank.

The campus bank may also promise that loan refunds will be credited to your account quickly. But the school must offer a number of ways to get the money to you, including direct deposit to any account in your name. So that's not a compelling reason for your choice.

How Can I Give Back?

Money's Great. But It's Not the Only Way to Help.

Giving to charitable causes, even ones that you care about a lot, can seem impossible on a limited budget. But before you abandon the idea of chipping in, remember that it's not only money that can make a difference—you can give your time too.

If you do feel strongly about actually giving money, you can include donations to a philanthropic organization as an item in your budget. But check if that will push the budget into the red. If so, then it's time to cut back on some other expenses to make sure you have enough to put towards that donation goal.

As an example, if you'd like to be able to give $25 a month to the

 **GIVING YOUR TIME**

It's true that financial donations can go a long way towards helping others and reaching specific goals, such as rebuilding a school after an earthquake or providing Thanksgiving dinners to homeless families. And it can be a great feeling to give money to a worthy cause (rather than spending it on yourself). **But your donated time, energy, and creativity are equally powerful resources.** Just like financial donations, donations of time can be given in increments of practically any size, from an hour here and there to a major part of your schedule.

A few ideas for giving time might include:

- Spending a spring break in an area that has been devastated by a natural disaster, rebuilding schools or homes

- Teaching kids at a local community center once a week—soccer, painting, computers—whatever you're good at

- Organizing a clothing or food drive in your dorm or house, or even campus-wide, to donate to a local shelter or community group

- Getting involved in a campus group that supports a cause you believe in. It could be a campus chapter of an environmental group, a group raising money for refugees, or tutoring members of the community

local animal shelter, or $100 to an organization that helps international refugees, skipping a few dinners out at a restaurant, or waiting until the new running shoes you want are on sale, should go a long way towards getting you to that goal.

Heads Up: Choose the Right Charity

Before you give money to a specific charity, it's always a must to make sure it is legitimate—and worthy. You can go to charitynavigator.org or guidestar.org to research an organization and make sure that it gets a good overall rating—meaning that your money is being put to use the way you'd imagined. There are other charity rating websites out there, but many of them charge you to use their services. There's no need to pay those fees—that's money that could be going directly to your chosen charity. *(See Resources)*

⭐ BEING A VOLUNTEER HELPS YOU TOO

While it's fairly obvious that serving as a volunteer is a huge help to the organizations to which you're donating your time, there are lots of ways that volunteering benefits you too:

- Avoid fees and costs. For example, if you volunteer as an usher for a concert, you can almost always stay and enjoy the music, without having to buy a ticket.

- Enrich your learning experience. Volunteering in a lab, a classroom, or for a performing arts production gives you excellent hands-on experience. It's almost like getting extra classes for free.

- Help your resume shine. Showing that you've spent time as a volunteer can help prospective employers take notice of your interests, your work ethic, and your commitment to helping others.

It's a great way to make connections. Not only will you meet other students and maybe professors who are interested in the same things you are, but it can help you form connections that can be useful when you're looking for a job, during school and after you graduate.

AND SPEAKING OF JOBS...

You may be able to translate your interest in helping others into a salaried job. Public service jobs, which include jobs working for the government, for non-profit organizations, or for Americorps or the PeaceCorps, can be the start of a great career path. Even better, these types of jobs are one way to loan forgiveness.

What are the requirements for loan forgiveness?

1. Your loan has to be a Direct Loan from the Federal Government.

2. You have to work at least 30 hours a week for a qualifying employer, which includes those listed above and others.

3. You have to make at least 120 qualifying payments before the loan is forgiven. That means it will take 10 years of payments (but that's about half the average time it takes students who get a Bachelor's degree to pay off their loans).

MAJOR MONEY MOMENT

GO GREEN

Personal responsibility, and small actions, can make a big difference when it comes to saving energy and money. There are a number of colleges that take this very seriously. One is Bowling Green State University, where there is an energy-saving team of students who walk the whole campus on Friday nights, making sure all the classroom lights are turned off. Not only does this save the college money. It also significantly reduces its energy consumption.

Your college might have some green initiatives that could use your help. Or you could follow this example and make sure to turn off the lights in your own room, dorm, or apartment. While you're at it, unplugging unused chargers, shutting down computers, and making sure faucets aren't dripping just take a second, but can make a world of difference for the planet.

Resources

BUDGETING

Mint
mint.com

PocketGuard
pocketguard.com

Slice
slice.com

Wally
wally.me

CREDIT

Annual Credit Report
Annualcreditreport.com

myFico
myfico.com

FEDERAL GRANTS

General grant Information
Studentaid.gov

Federal Pell Grants
studentaid.ed.gov/sa/types/
grants-scholarships/pell

Teacher Education Assistance for College and Higher Education (TEACH) Grant
studentaid.ed.gov/sa/types/
grants-scholarships/fseog

FINANCIAL AID

Consumer Finance Protection Bureau
http://www.consumerfinance.gov/
paying-for-college

Financial Aid ToolKit
https://financialaidtoolkit.ed.gov/tk/
resources/all.jsp

NASFAA
https://www.nasfaa.org/Students_
Parents_Counselors

State Financial Aid
https://www.nasfaa.org/State_
Financial_Aid_Programs

Your school's financial aid office

Your school's Bursar's office

LOANS

General loan information
Studentaid.gov

Direct Loans
studentaid.ed.gov/sa/types/loans

Perkins Loans
studentaid.ed.gov/sa/types/loans/
perkins

LOAN REPAYMENT

General repayment information
studentaid.ed.gov/sa/
repay-loans/understand/plans

Repayment Estimator
studentloans.gov/
myDirectLoan/mobile/repayment/
repaymentEstimator.action

PHILANTHROPY

Charity Navigator
Charitynavigator.com

GuideStar
Guidestar.org

SCHOLARSHIPS

General scholarship information
Scholarships.com

TIME BUDGETING

Tick
tickspot.com

MyMinutes
www.myminutesapp.com/

RESEARCH

Learning While Earning
(Georgetown University)
https://cew.georgetown.edu/
cew-reports/workinglearners/

Friday Night Lights
https://www.bgsu.edu/campus-
sustainability/energy/friday-
night-lights.html

GENERAL MONEY MANAGEMENT

CashCourse
CashCourse.org

My Money
MyMoney.gov

Susan Beacham is CEO of Money Savvy Generation (msgen.com) and creator of the award-winning Money Savvy Pig—a 21st century bank that teaches kids about money choice. Susan is an award-winning education entrepreneur and nationally recognized kids and money expert. She is also the co-author of the award-winning children's book series, the *Money Savvy Kids Club* book series, as well as the Parents' Choice Gold Award Winner *O.M.G. Official Money Guide for Teenagers*. She is also the creator of the innovative iPhone App for

kids—Savings Spree—a Parents' Choice Gold Award winner and Editor's Choice winner by Children's Technology Review. Prior to founding Money Savvy Generation, Susan spent 18 years working in financial services with senior management positions at Northern Trust, Wells Fargo and Bank of America. Follow Susan's advice on her blog at susanbeacham.com.

Michael Beacham is an expert in financial services and financial education for youth. He co-founded the pioneering financial education company, Money Savvy Generation, with his wife, Susan in 1999. Together with Susan he co-authored the award-winning *Money Savvy Kids Basic Personal Finance Curriculum* and the *Money Savvy U Intermediate Personal Finance Curriculum*, as well as the Parents' Choice Gold Award Winner *O.M.G. Official Money Guide for Teenagers*. He also served as editor of the *Money Savvy Kids Club* book series. Michael

led the development of the award-winning children's financial literacy game *Savings Spree*, available for iOS devices. Prior to founding Money Savvy Generation, Michael spent 18 years working in international financial services with senior management positions in the U.S. and abroad with Northern Trust, KPMG Consulting and Accenture.

Allison Beacham is a writer and blogger. A 2014 graduate of Miami University, with a degree in creative writing, Allison works in sales for a Chicago-based products company. In her spare time, when she's not working on her screenplay, she writes the gluten-free lifestyle blog lifesabeacham.com. Allison was in the very first cohort of first grade students educated by Money Savvy Generation and proudly calls herself a founding member of the money-savvy generation.

ACKNOWLEDGMENTS

To Jane Clinard, Admissions Program Coordinator, Bowling Green State University, for her dedication to creating a financially empowered generation and for her help and guidance with this book.

Special thanks to our editor Mavis Wright and our development partner, Lightbulb Press.

©2016 Money Savvy Generation, Inc. All rights reserved.

825 S. Waukegan Rd., Ste A8 PMB 137
Lake Forest, IL 60045
1-866-390-5959

www.msgen.com

ISBN: 978-0-9842139-5-5